THE BEST FILM SCORES

2 Composers featured in this collection—biographies, highlighted lists of works

THE MUSIC:

ISBN 0-634-01717-9

HAL•LEONARD®
CORPORATION

7777 W. BLUEMOUND RD. P.O. BOX 13819 MILWAUKEE, WI 53213

Visit Hal Leonard Online at
www.halleonard.com

COMPOSERS FEATURED IN THIS COLLECTION

JOHN BARRY

Born in York, England on November 3, 1933, John Barry Prendergast was first introduced to the world of films as a projectionist in his father's movie theaters. After playing trumpet in a British Army band, Barry formed the John Barry Seven in 1957, with whom he performed and recorded extensively. In 1959 he began writing for film, television shows and commercials, serving for a time as the musical director and arranger for EMI Records. Barry's big break came in 1962 when he was asked to work on the first James Bond movie, *Dr. No*. The success of this project, specifically of "The James Bond Theme," got Barry the job of scoring the next eleven Bond films. Even though he is equally adept at jazz, classical and popular styles, it is his melodic gift that his fans treasure. That gift is fully in evidence in one of his most beloved scores, *Dances with Wolves*.

Selected film scores: *Dr. No* (uncredited co-composer with Monty Norman) (1962), *Born Free*** (1966), *The Lion in Winter*** (1968), *Mary, Queen of Scots** (1971), *Robin and Marian* (1976), *Body Heat* (1981), *Out of Africa*** (1985), *Dances with Wolves*** (1990), *Chaplin** (1992).

GEORGES DELERUE

Born in Roubaix, France in 1925, Delerue was the son of working-class parents. Originally, he pursued music lessons to qualify for an exemption from military service, but began composing in earnest during long months of hospitalization following a spinal cord injury. After the end of the war he entered the Paris Conservatory to further his studies. His many compositions for the concert hall have won a number of awards and prizes. He once said that his concert and film music were like "two languages with the same basis." He died in California on March 20, 1992. "The Friendship Theme" from *Beaches*, presented in this folio, underscores the deep, but often turbulent, friendship between the women played by Bette Midler and Barbara Hershey.

Selected film scores: *Hiroshima, Mon Amour* (1959), *Shoot the Piano Player* (1960), *Jules and Jim* (1961), *The Pumpkin Eater* (1964), *A Man for All Seasons* (1966), *Anne of a Thousand Days** (1969), *The Day of the Dolphin** (1973), *Julia** (1977), *A Little Romance*** (1979), *Agnes of God** (1985), *Beaches* (1988).

PATRICK DOYLE

Doyle was born on April 6, 1953 near Glasgow. He learned tuba and piano before studying at the Royal Scottish Academy of Music and Drama. After graduation Doyle worked for twelve years as an actor and composer for British television. He joined Kenneth Branagh's Renaissance Theatre Company in 1987 as actor, composer, and musical director, writing music for a large number of productions. His career in film scoring began in 1989 when he was asked to write the music for Branagh's new film of Shakespeare's *Henry V*. Since then Doyle has composed more than twenty scores for a variety of films, including other period pieces, horror films, and Mafia crime thrillers.

Selected film scores: *Henry V* (1989), *Much Ado About Nothing* (1993), *Frankenstein* (1994), *Sense and Sensibilty** (1995), *Hamlet** (1996), *Donnie Brasco* (1997), *Great Expectations* (1998), *Love's Labour's Lost* (2000).

JERRY GOLDSMITH

Jerry Goldsmith's trademark is diversity. His work is strikingly different from one motion picture to the next. He is comfortable using diverse instruments, sounds and compositional approaches, and is equally at home with symphony orchestras and the latest in electronic hardware. He was born in Los Angeles on February 10, 1929. He attended the film composition classes given by Miklós Rózsa at USC, and first composed scores for CBS radio. Graduating to television in 1955, Goldsmith wrote acclaimed scores for such hit TV series as "Thriller," "The Man from U.N.C.L.E." and "The Twilight Zone." Goldsmith's list of scores for motion pictures starts in the year 1957, and reads like an honor roll of Hollywood films. The two themes featured here show his wide compositional range—the sleazy film noire atmosphere of *Chinatown* and the majestic, epic splendor of *Star Trek®—The Motion Picture* (which was later utilized for the "Star Trek—The Next Generation" television series).

Selected film scores: *Freud** (1963), *A Patch of Blue** (1965), *The Sand Pebbles** (1966), *Planet of the Apes** (1968), *Patton** (1970), *Papillon** (1973), *QB VII* (1974 - Television mini-series; Emmy Award), *Chinatown** (1974), *The Wind and the Lion** (1975), *The Omen*** (1976), *The Boys from Brazil** (1978), *Star Trek®—The Motion Picture** (1979), *Poltergeist** (1982), *Under Fire** (1983), *Hoosiers** (1986), *Basic Instinct** (1992), *The River Wild* (1994), *Mulan** (1998).

DAVE GRUSIN

Dave Grusin first established himself as a jazz pianist. He began writing scores for television and graduated to features in the late '60s. Born on June 26, 1934, he was generally identified with comedy when he was asked to do the dramatic underscore to *The Graduate*, his big break. In addition to his work in film, he has written several acclaimed compositions for symphony orchestra, and still records for GRP Records, a label he co-owned until its recent sale to MCA. The wide range of his scores show why he is so respected and in demand.

Selected film scores: *The Graduate* (1967), *Heaven Can Wait** (1978), *The Champ** (1979), *On Golden Pond** (1981), *Tootsie* (1982), *The Milagro Beanfield War*** (1988), *The Fabulous Baker Boys** (1989), *Havana** (1990), *The Firm** (1993).

BERNARD HERRMANN

Born on June 30, 1911, Herrmann studied the violin at an early age. But his real love was conducting, and by age twenty, he created and conducted the New Chamber Orchestra. In 1934, he went to work for CBS radio, where he served as an arranger and composer. It was his work on Orson Welles' radio shows that first brought him out to Hollywood to write the scores for *Citizen Kane* and *The Magnificent Ambersons*. He wrote memorable music for many films, and between 1955 and 1965, wrote the music to all of Alfred Hitchcock's motion pictures. He lived in London in the '70s, conducting albums of his film scores, concert works, and music by neglected composers. He died in Los Angeles on December 24, 1975, right after completing the music to *Taxi Driver*. This score was the first time he utilized jazz elements in his writing, a direction that he would have continued to explore had he lived. *Psycho* is one of the classic suspense scores of all times, and once heard is not forgotten.

Selected film scores: *Citizen Kane** (1941), *All That Money Can Buy*** (1942), *The Magnificent Ambersons* (1942), *Anna and the King of Siam** (1946), *The Ghost and Mrs. Muir* (1947), *The Seventh Voyage of Sinbad* (1958), *Psycho* (1960), *Marnie* (1964), *Obsession** (1976), *Taxi Driver** (1976).

MAURICE JARRE

Jarre was born in Lyons, France on September 13, 1924. He wrote concert music and film scores in France when he received a call from director David Lean to write the score to *Lawrence of Arabia*. The incredible success of this score catapulted Jarre to worldwide fame and many assignments. In addition to his orchestral scores, Jarre has become renowned for his electronic scores for such films as *Witness*. Both scores to *Ghost* and *Fatal Attraction* have become cult classics.

Selected film scores: *Lawrence of Arabia*** (1962), *Doctor Zhivago*** (1965), *Ryan's Daughter* (1970), *Mohammed, Messenger of God** (1974), *The Tin Drum* (1979), *A Passage to India*** (1984), *Witness** (1984), *Fatal Attraction* (1987), *Gorillas in the Mist** (1988), *Ghost** (1990).

HENRY MANCINI

Mancini was born on April 16, 1924 in Cleveland, Ohio. His father taught him to play the flute, and young Henry learned to write arrangements from Max Adkins in Pittsburgh, Pennsylvania. After service in World War II, Mancini joined the Glenn Miller Orchestra as arranger and pianist. In 1951, he joined the composing staff of Universal Pictures where he remained until 1958. His break came when producer Blake Edwards asked him to write the music for the television show "Peter Gunn." Mancini recorded the music for an album, and the album became a best-seller. *Breakfast at Tiffany's* won for Mancini his first of many Oscars for Best Score or Song. A successful composer of film scores (his descriptive "Baby Elephant Walk" not only enhanced the action in the film, but was a million-selling record), concert music and pop songs, Mancini also became a concert conductor and TV personality. He was completing the score for the Broadway show *Victor/Victoria* when he died on June 14, 1994 in Los Angeles.

Selected film scores: *The Glenn Miller Story** (co-composer - 1954), *Breakfast at Tiffany's*** (1961), *Days of Wine and Roses* (1962), *Hatari!* (1962), *The Pink Panther** (1964), *Charade* (1964), *Sunflower** (1969), *The Molly Maguires* (1970), *10** (1979), *Victor/Victoria*** (1984), *The Glass Menagerie* (1987).

ENNIO MORRICONE

One of the most prolific composers in film music history, Morricone was born in Rome on October 11, 1928. His earliest scores were Italian light comedies and costume pictures, where Morricone learned to write simple, memorable themes. His themes for such films as *A Fistful of Dollars, For a Few Dollars More* and *The Good, the Bad and the Ugly* became best-selling records. He writes music for films produced all over the world. *The Mission, The Untouchables* and the poetic *Cinema Paradiso* are three of his most beloved scores.

Selected film scores: *A Fistful of Dollars* (1964), *For a Few Dollars More* (1965), *The Good, the Bad and the Ugly* (1966), *Once Upon a Time in the West* (1969), *Exorcist II: The Heretic* (1977), *Days of Heaven** (1978), *Once Upon a Time in America* (1985), *The Mission** (1986), *The Untouchables** (1987), *Cinema Paradiso* (1989), *The Legend of 1900* (1999).

NINO ROTA

Born in Milan, Italy on December 31, 1911, Rota was a prodigy in music, composing large-scale orchestral works, and even an opera, while he was still in his teens. He studied at the Milan Conservatory with Alfredo Casella, and the Curtis Institute of Music in the United States. His professional relationships with the great Italian directors such as Federico Fellini (*Amarcord, 8 1/2, La dolce vita*), Luchino Visconti (*The Leopard*), and Franco Zeffirelli *(Romeo and Juliet)* allowed him to write some of the finest film music ever composed. Perhaps his greatest success was the music for the Francis Ford Coppola *Godfather* trilogy. Rota died in Rome on April 10, 1979.

Selected film scores: *I Vitelloni* (1953), *La Strada* (1954), *War and Peace* (1956), *Nights of Cabiria* (1957), *La dolce vita* (1960), *Rocco and His Brothers* (1960), 8 1/2 (1963), *The Leopard* (1963), *Juliet of the Spirits* (1965), *Romeo and Juliet* (1968), *The Godfather* (1972), *The Godfather, Part II*** (co-composed with Carmine Coppola) (1974).

MIKLÓS RÓZSA

Like other Hungarian composers such as Bela Bartok and Zoltan Kodaly, Rózsa's music is imbued with the folk music of his native land. Born in Budapest, Hungary on April 18, 1907, Rózsa studied the violin as a child, later taking up the piano. Formal music training continued in Leipzig in the late '20s, and in 1932, Rózsa settled in Paris. As his reputation as a concert composer grew, he began writing background music for documentaries and newsreels. Eventually he attracted the attention of producer Alexander Korda, and began his film score career in earnest in the late '30s in England. Moving to Hollywood in 1940, his scores for Paramount, Selznick and MGM became instant classics. *Spellbound*, in particular, was tremendously popular, featuring the unusual instrument, the theramin. Rózsa taught for many years at USC, conducted many concerts at the Hollywood Bowl, and continued his composition of concert music almost until his death in 1995.

Selected film scores: *The Thief of Baghdad** (1940), *Jungle Book** (1942), *Double Indemnity** (1944), *The Lost Weekend** (1945), *Spellbound*** (1945), *The Killers** (1946), *A Double Life*** (1947), *Quo Vadis** (1951), *Ivanhoe** (1952), *Julius Caesar** (1953), *Ben Hur*** (1959), *El Cid** (1961), *Time after Time* (1979).

ALAN SILVESTRI

Born in New York on March 20, 1950, Silvestri was raised in Teaneck, New Jersey. He attended Berklee College and played in rock bands upon graduation. He wrote the music for the television show "CHiPS," and helped out writing some cues for the film *Romancing the Stone*. The director of the film was so impressed, he asked Silvestri to write the entire score. The director was Robert Zemeckis (who later made *Back to the Future* and *Forrest Gump*), and the score launched Silvestri's career.

Selected film scores: *Romancing the Stone* (1984), *Back to the Future* trilogy (1985, 1989, 1990), *Who Framed Roger Rabbit?* (1988), *The Abyss* (1989), *Grumpy Old Men* (1993), *Forrest Gump* (1994).

VANGELIS

(Vangelis Odyssey Papathanoussiou)

Born in Valos, Greece on March 29, 1943, Vangelis was a child prodigy, performing publicly on the piano at the age of six. He moved to France and was a member of the group Aphrodite's Child with vocalist Demis Rousos. When the group disbanded, Vangelis moved to London. His recordings with Jon Anderson of the group Yes were praised in music magazines and sold well. Vangelis' score for *Chariots of Fire* made him an international star, and the soundtrack album continues to be a best-seller.

Selected film scores: *Chariots of Fire*** (1981), *Blade Runner* (1982), *Missing* (1982), *The Bounty* (1984), *1492: Conquest of Paradise* (1992).

JOHN WILLIAMS

After years of being out of fashion, the lush, romantic, sweeping full-orchestral score made a major comeback in John Towner Williams' score for the blockbuster *Star Wars*. Pretty good for a classically trained pianist who first became known as a jazz player and arranger. Williams was born in Flushing, New York on February 8, 1932, the son of Johnny Williams, for years a drummer on staff at CBS radio. Besides playing jazz piano, Williams played in many studio orchestras, and eventually broke into series television in the late '50s. After years of scoring musicals, light comedies and disaster movies, Williams scored a major success in 1975 with *Jaws*. Just one year later, *Star Wars* made him the number one composer in Hollywood. Its soundtrack album became the biggest-selling symphonic film score in history. Such themes as "E.T. (The Extra-Terrestrial)," "Raiders March," and the theme from *Schindler' List* are staples at pops concerts all over the world. For many years, Williams conducted the Boston Pops, and became a familiar face via the orchestra's television broadcasts. He is the composer of several concert works, including symphonies, concertos and fanfares.

Selected film scores: (# indicates nomination for Best Song Score Adaptation category)

Goodbye, Mr. Chips#** (1969), *The Reivers** (1970), *Fiddler on the Roof*#** (1971), *Images** (1972), *The Poseidon Adventure** (1972), *The Towering Inferno** (1974), *Jaws*** (1975), *Star Wars*** (1976), *Close Encounters of the Third Kind** (1977), *Superman** (1978), *The Empire Strikes Back** (1980), *Indiana Jones* trilogy** (1981, 1984, 1989), *E.T. (The Extra-Terrestrial)*** (1982), *Return of the Jedi** (1983), *Born on the Fourth of July** (1989), *JFK** (1991), *Schindler's List*** (1993), *Seven Years in Tibet* (1997), *Saving Private Ryan** (1998), *The Phantom Menace** (1999), *Angela's Ashes* (1999).

GABRIEL YARED

Born in Beirut, Lebanon on October 7, 1949, Gabriel Yared has spent most of his career in France. The self-taught musician gave up law studies in 1971 and moved to Brazil, before settling in Paris in 1972. He began composing film scores in the late 1970s and quickly become one of the most respected composers in French cinema. Since then he has produced a steady stream of soundtracks, including several Hollywood films.

Selected film scores: *The English Patient*** (1996), *The Talented Mr. Ripley** (1999).

THE JOHN DUNBAR THEME
from DANCES WITH WOLVES

By JOHN BARRY

Moderately

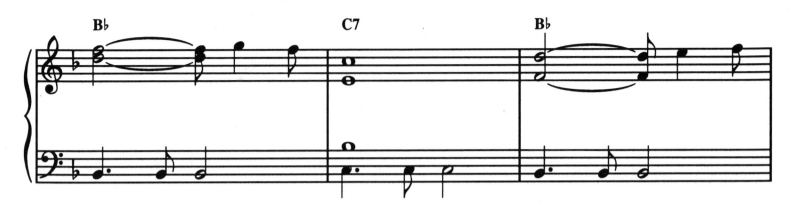

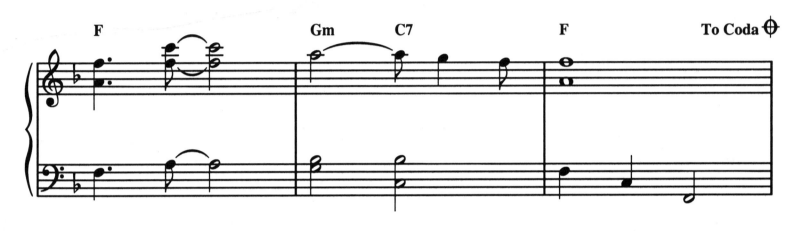

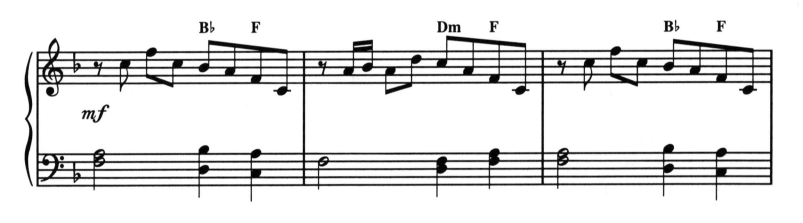

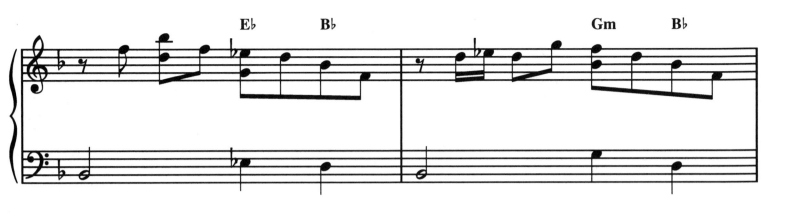

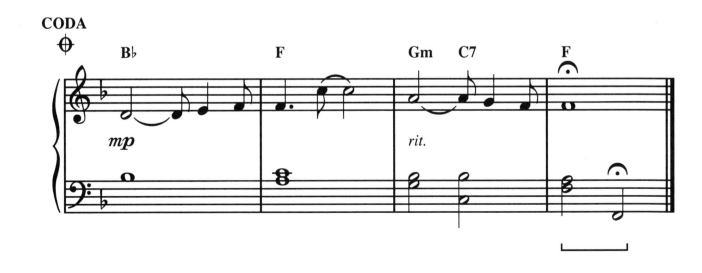

THE FRIENDSHIP THEME

from Touchstone Pictures' BEACHES

Music by GEORGES DELERUE

MY FATHER'S FAVORITE

from SENSE AND SENSIBILITY

By PATRICK DOYLE

Andante cantabile

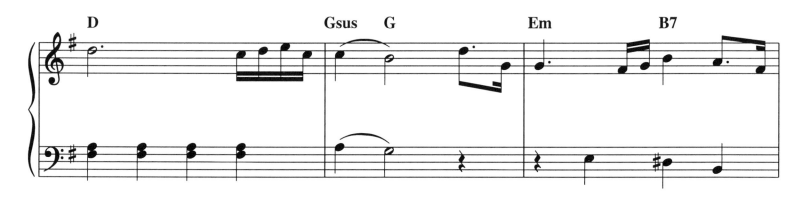

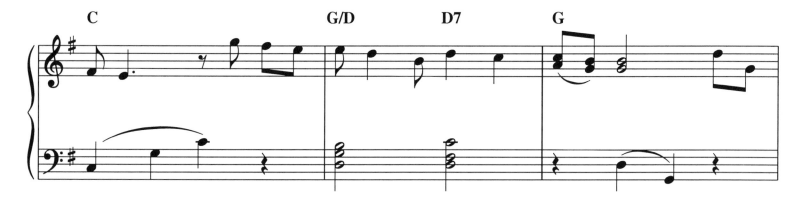

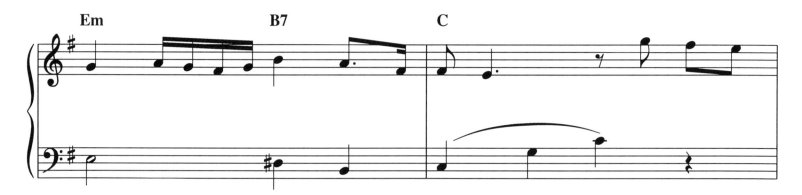

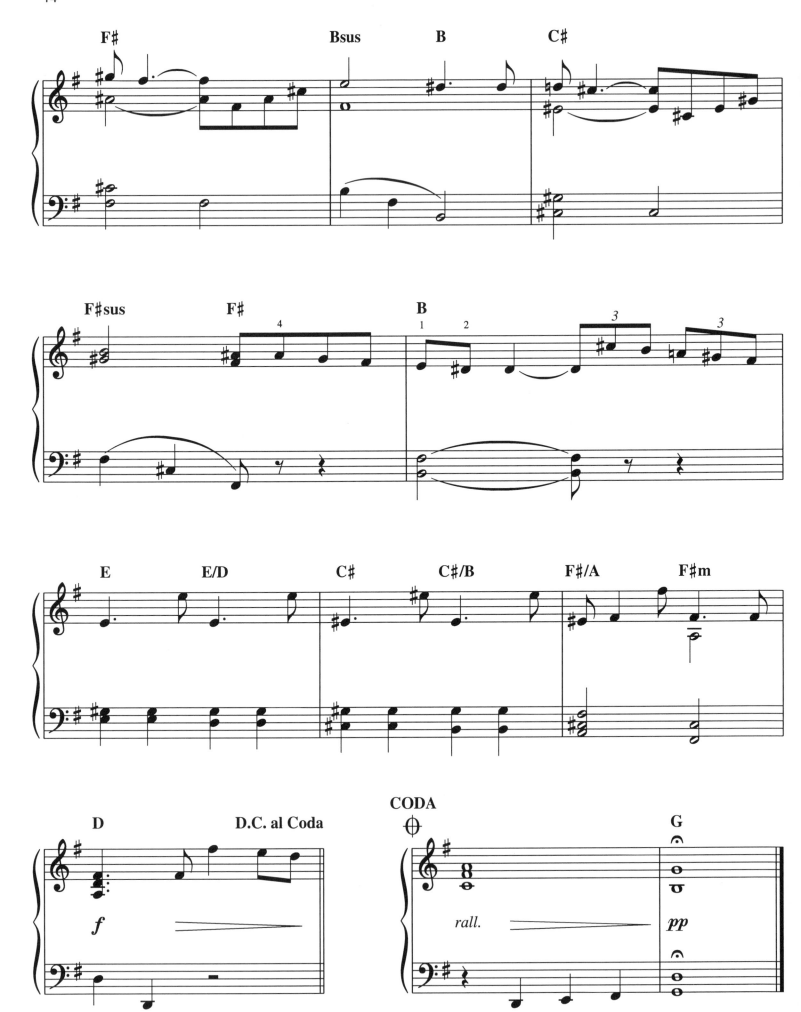

CHINATOWN
from the Paramount Motion Picture CHINATOWN

Music by JERRY GOLDSMITH

Moderately slow, flowing

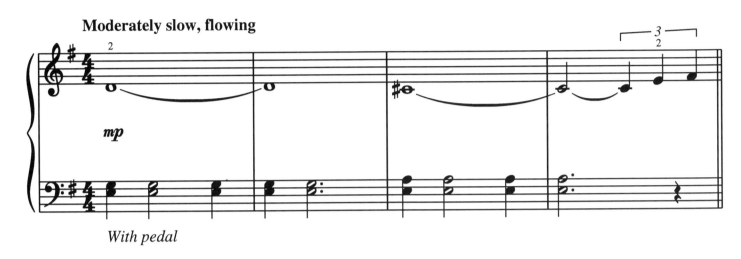

With pedal

STAR TREK® THE MOTION PICUTRE

Theme from the Paramount Picture STAR TREK: THE MOTION PICTURE

Music by JERRY GOLDSMITH

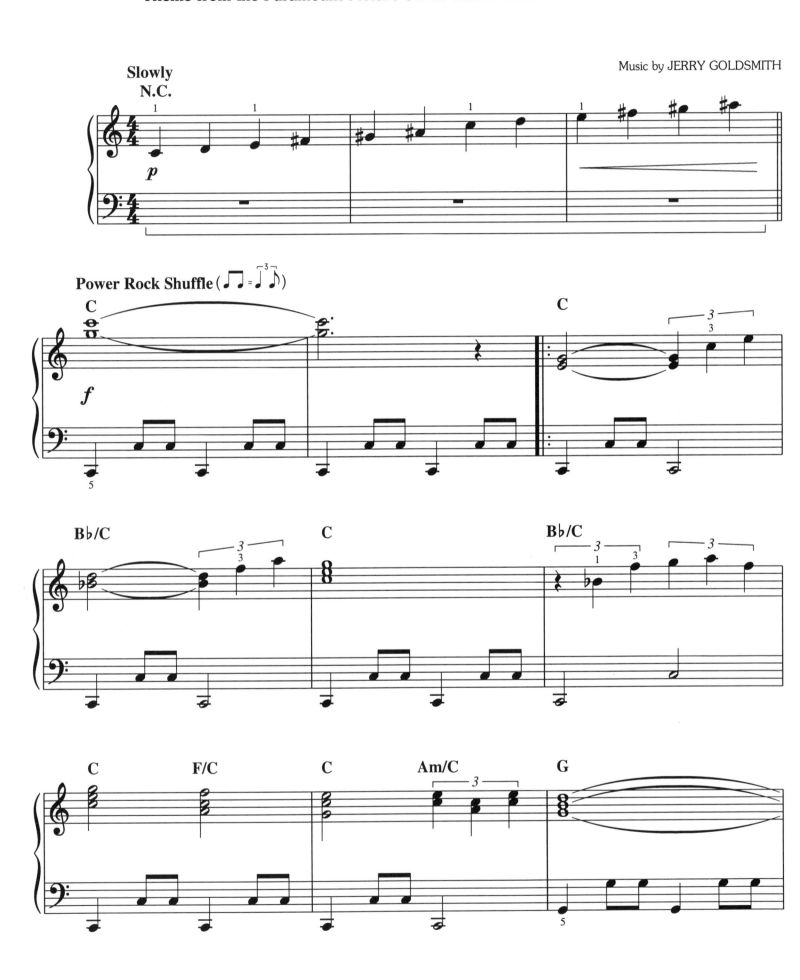

ON GOLDEN POND
Main Theme from ON GOLDEN POND

Very freely

Music by DAVE GRUSIN

p very delicately, as though from far away

Not fast, somewhat freely

22

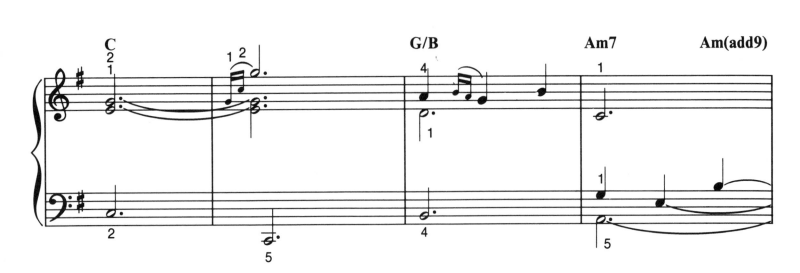

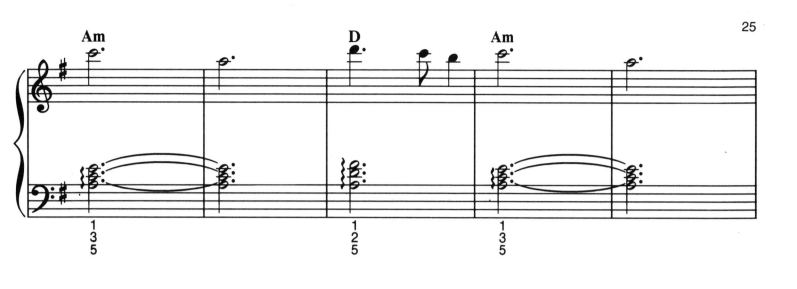

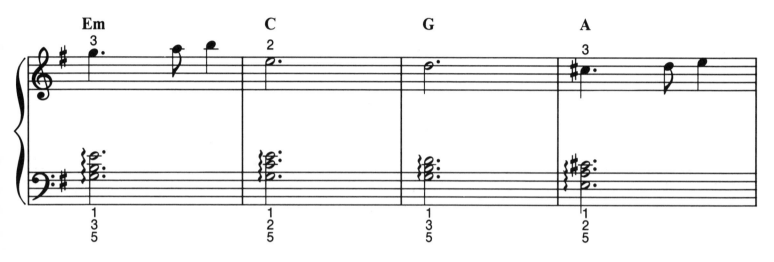

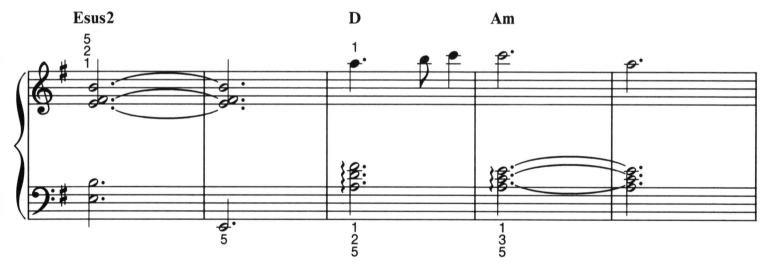

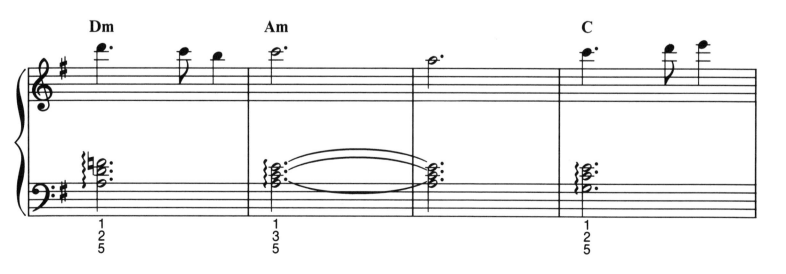

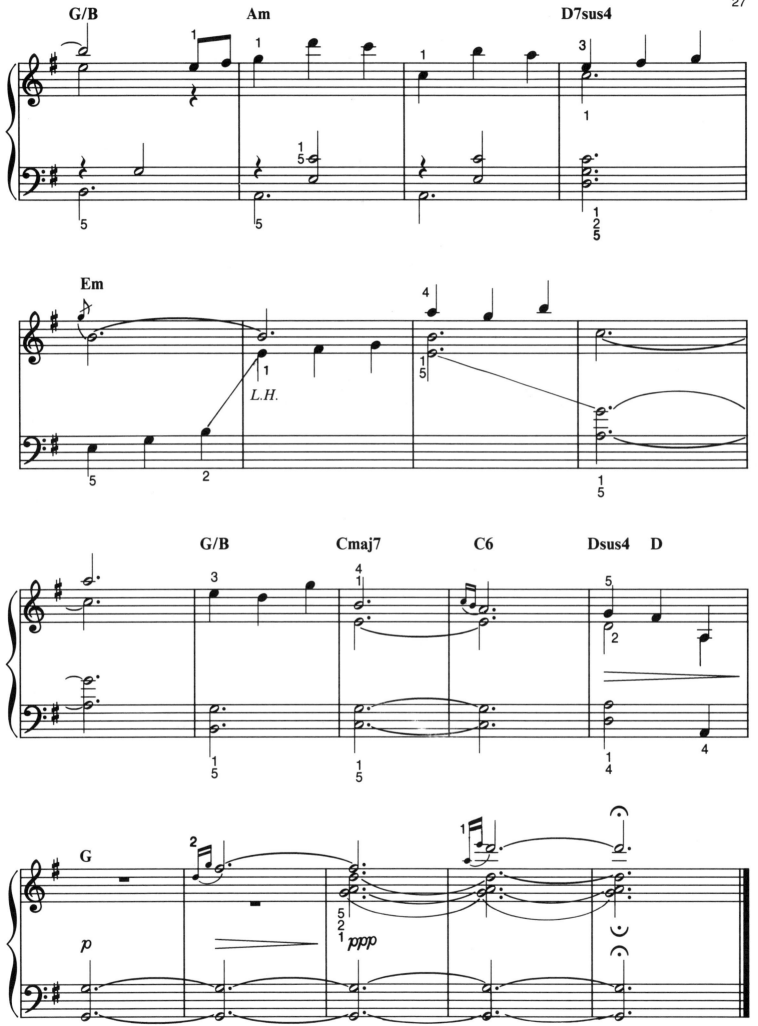

PSYCHO
(Prelude)
Theme from the Paramount Picture PSYCHO

Music by BERNARD HERRMANN

Slightly agitated, rhythmic

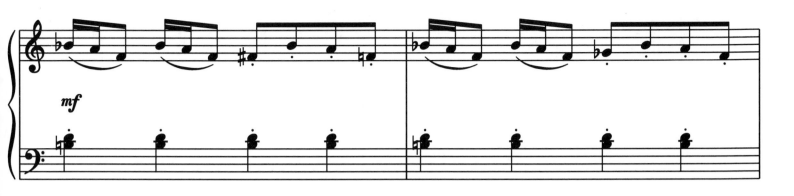

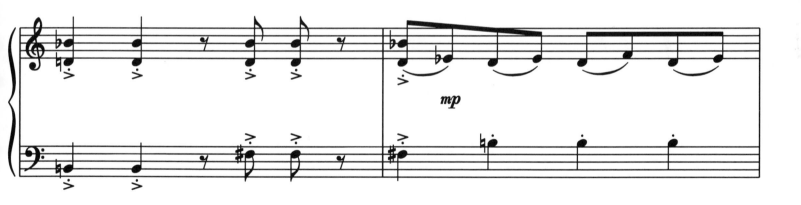

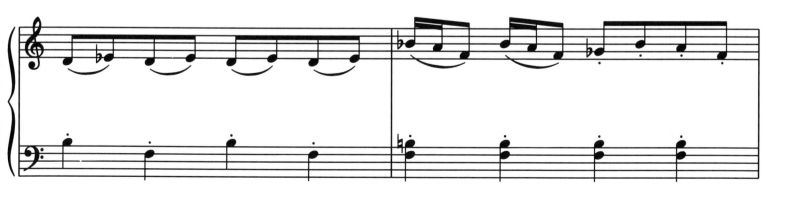

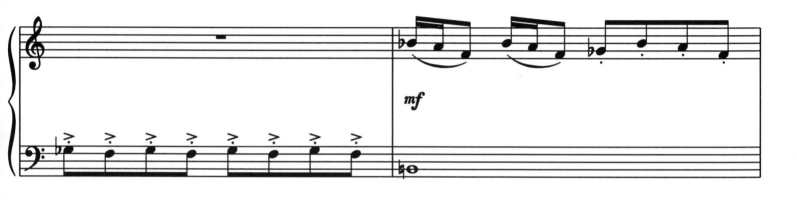

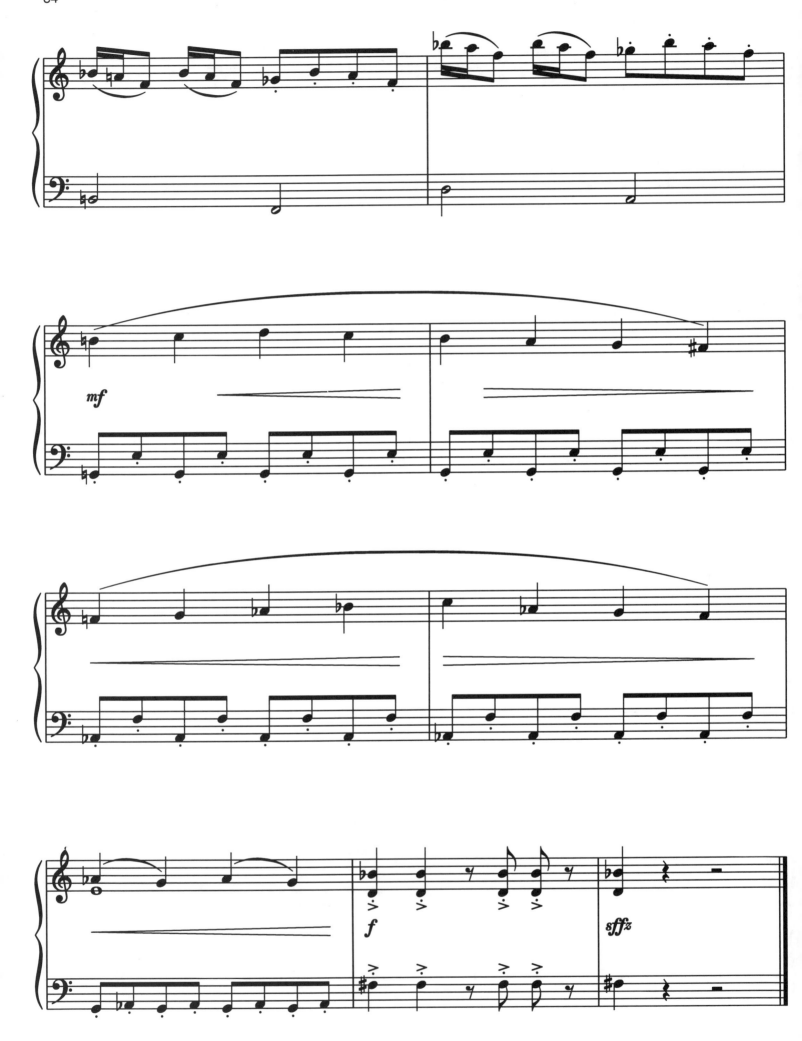

BREAKFAST AT TIFFANY'S

Theme from the Paramount Picture BREAKFAST AT TIFFANY'S

Music by HENRY MANCINI

TAXI DRIVER
(Theme)
from TAXI DRIVER

By BERNARD HERRMANN

Rubato, with expression and freedom

THEME FROM "LAWRENCE OF ARABIA"

from LAWRENCE OF ARABIA

By MAURICE JARRE

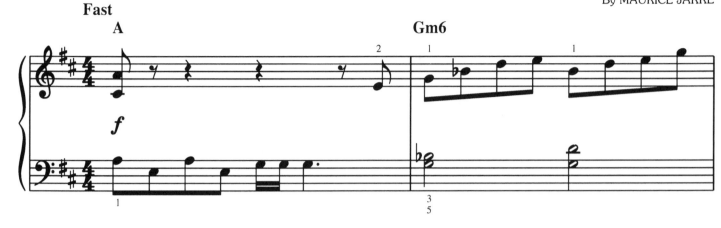

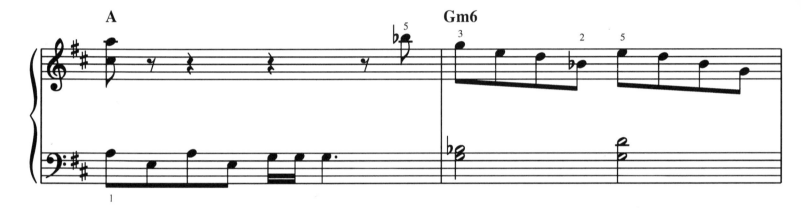

41

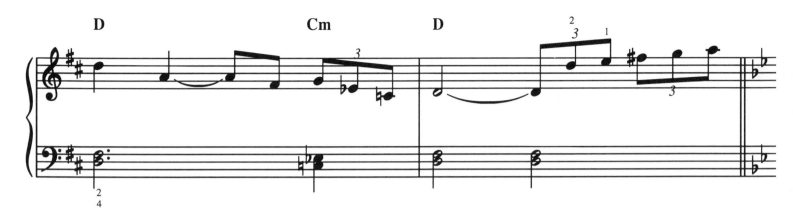

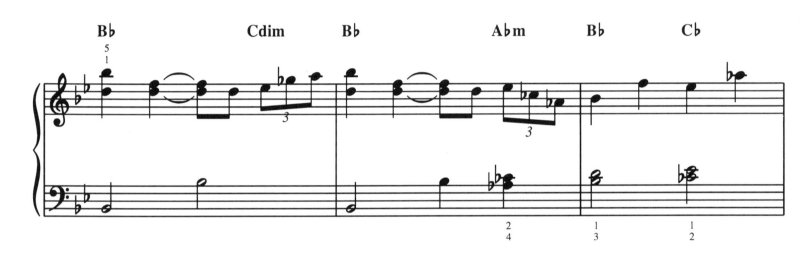

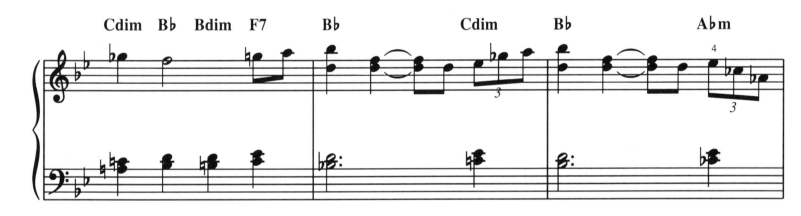

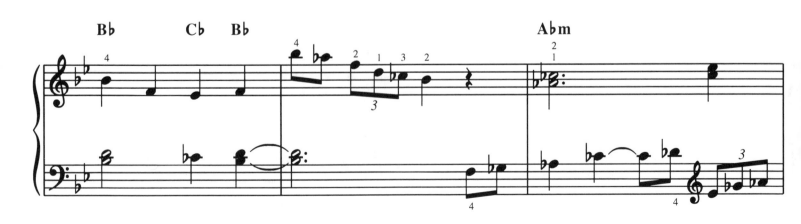

43

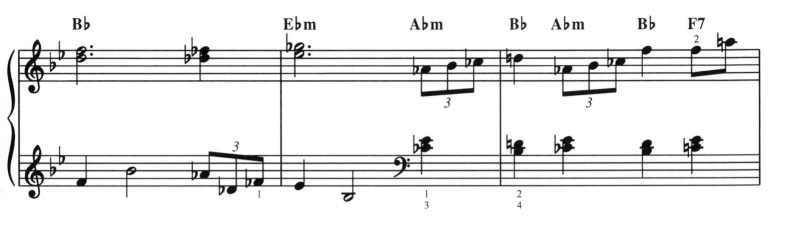

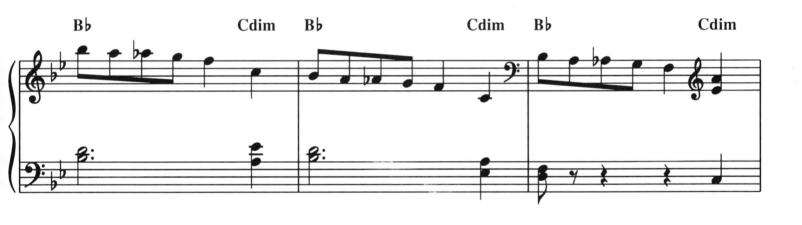

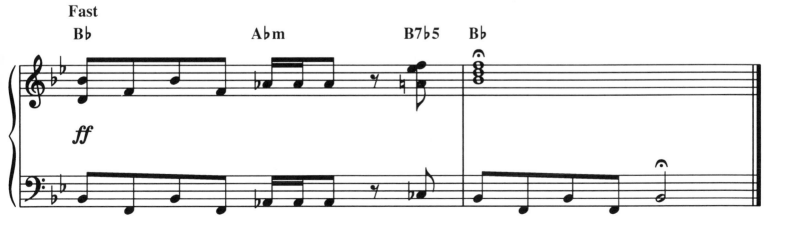

BABY ELEPHANT WALK

from the Paramount Picture HATARI!

By HENRY MANCINI

Moderately slow and steady

CINEMA PARADISO
from CINEMA PARADISO

Music by ENNIO MORRICONE

Moderately slow, with feeling

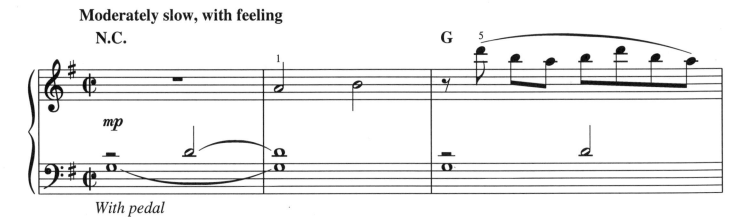

With pedal

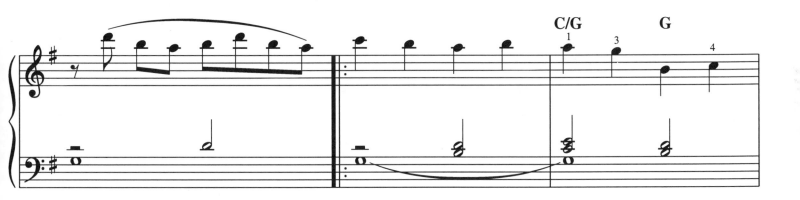

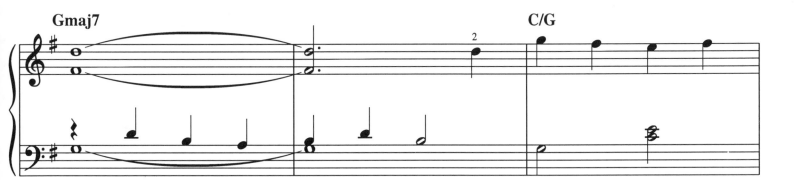

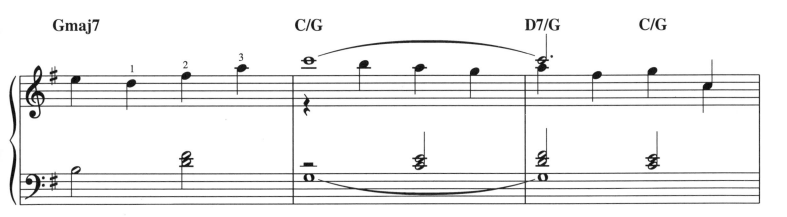

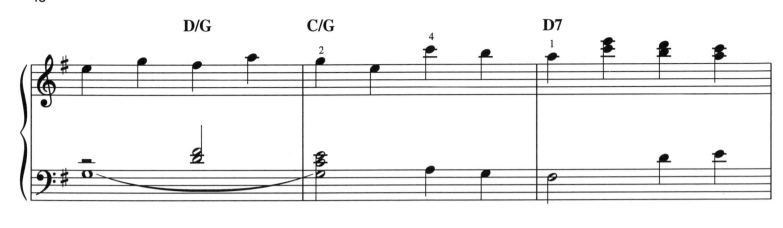

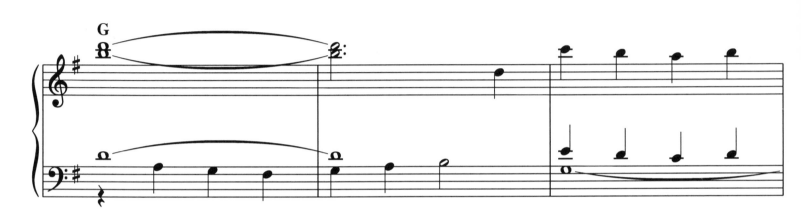

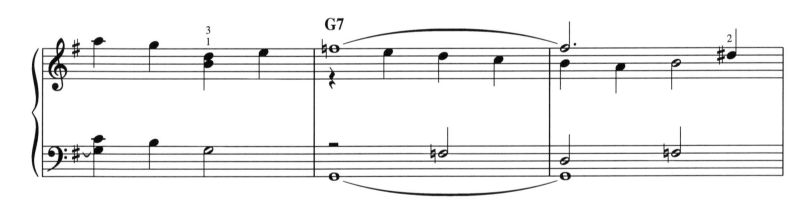

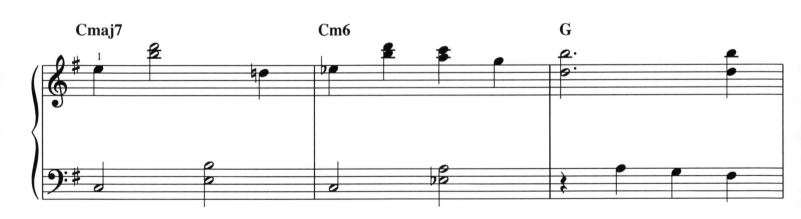

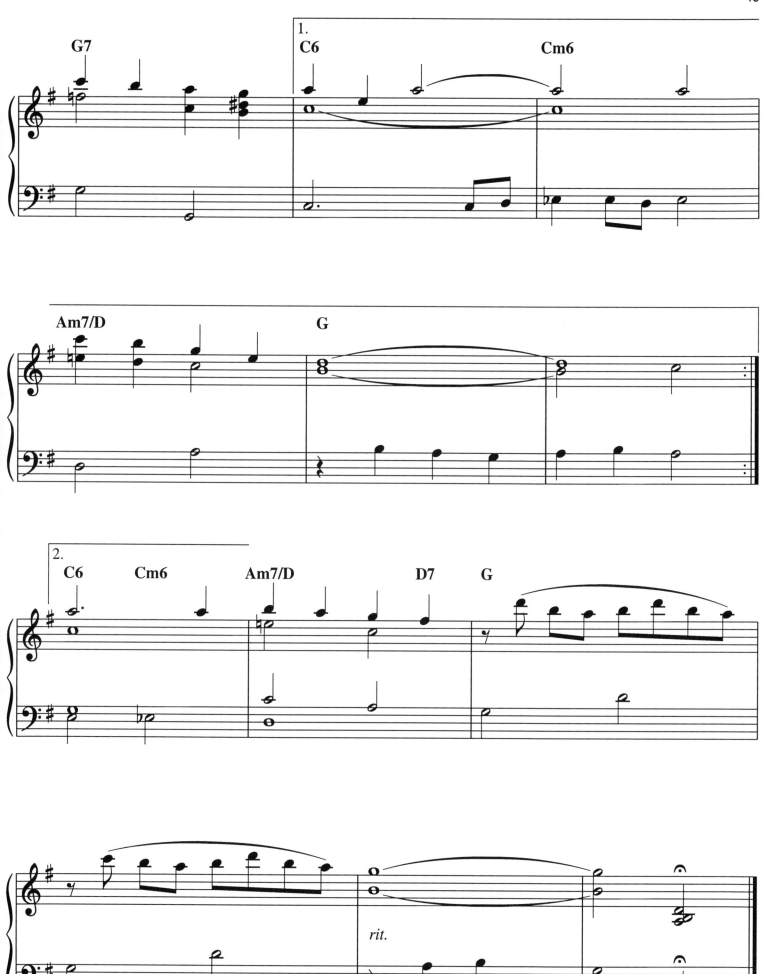

RIVER
from the Motion Picture THE MISSION

Music by ENNIO MORRICONE

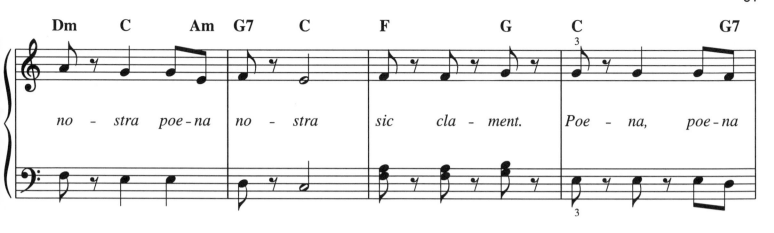

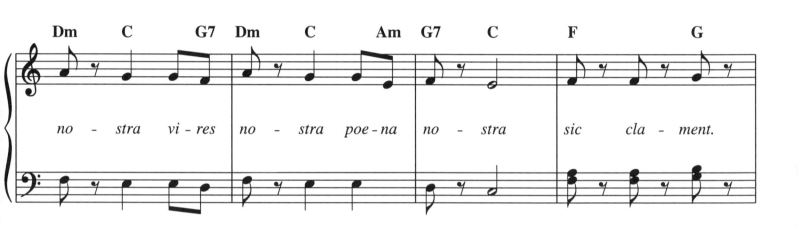

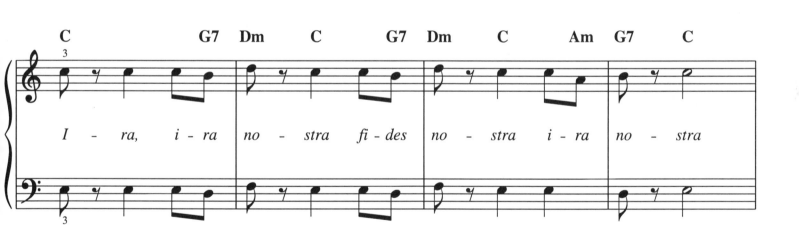

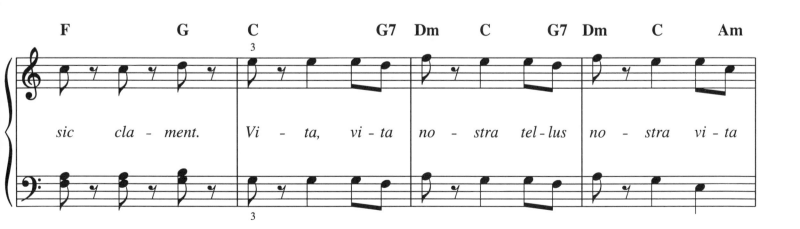

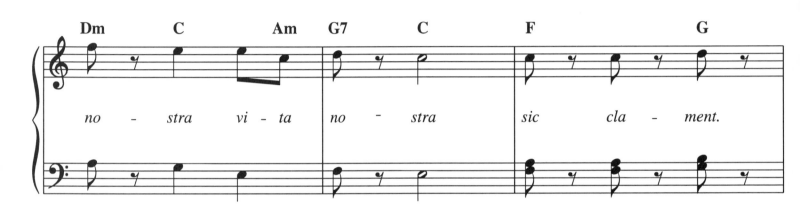

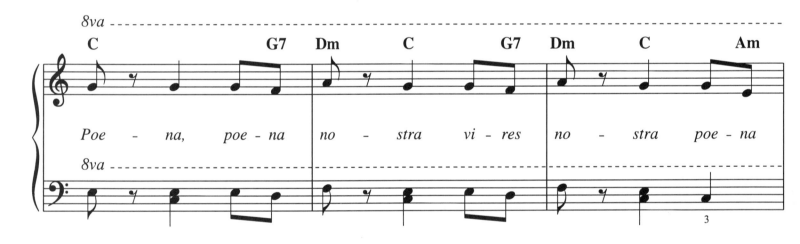

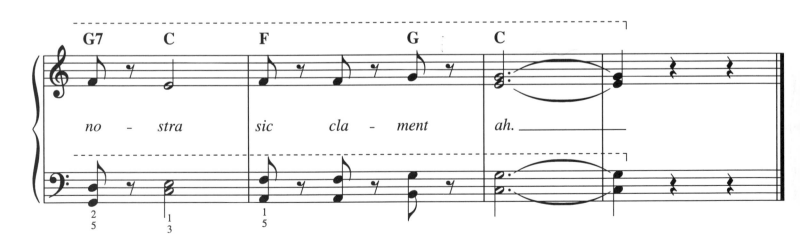

THE UNTOUCHABLES - MAIN TITLE

from the Paramount Motion Picture THE UNTOUCHABLES

Words and Music by
ENNIO MORRICONE

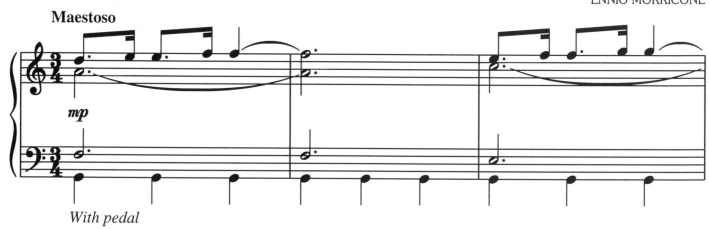

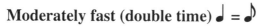

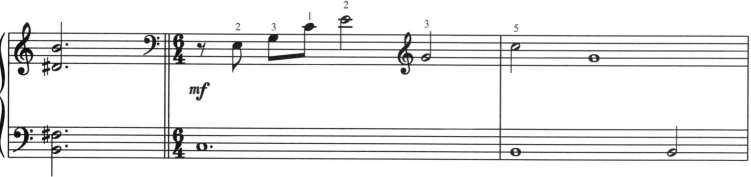

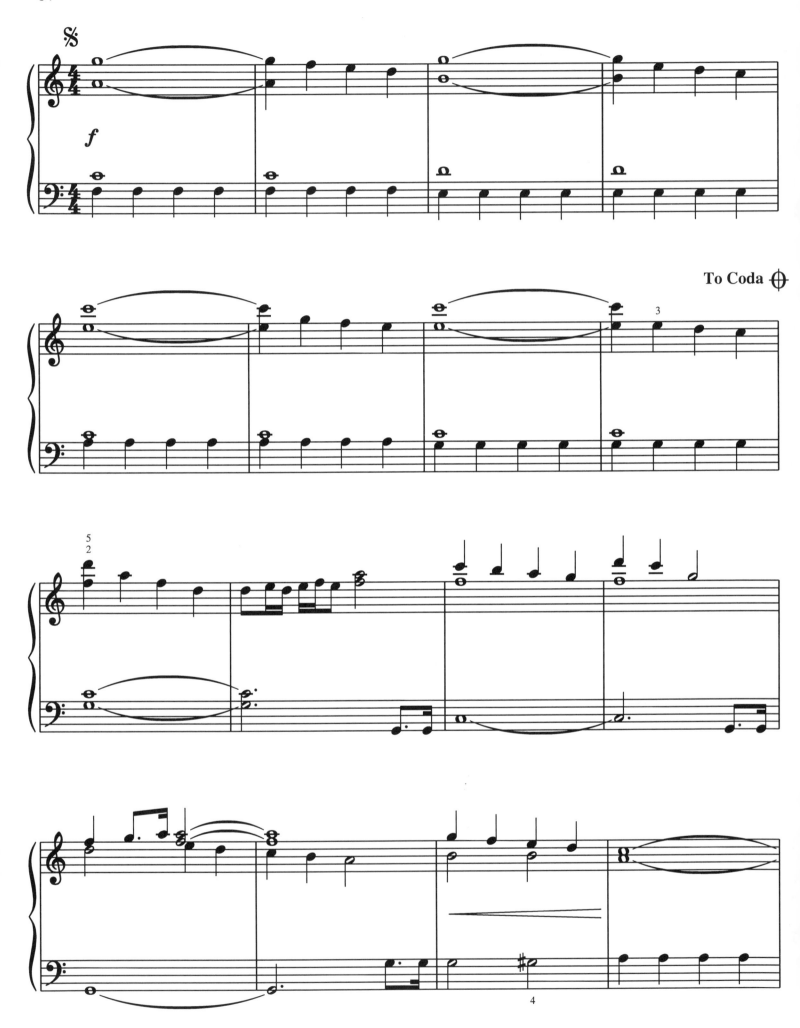

54

To Coda ⊕

D.S. al Coda

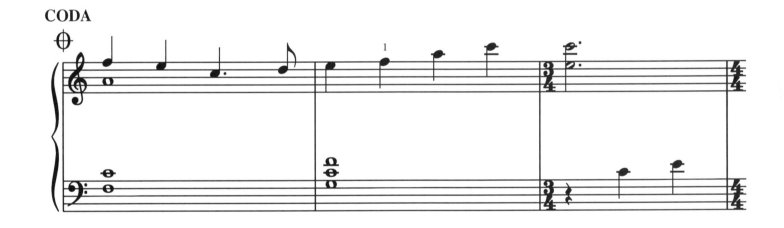

CODA

THE GODFATHER
(Love Theme)
from the Paramount Picture THE GODFATHER

By NINO ROTA

GODFATHER II
Theme from the Paramount Picture GODFATHER II

By NINO ROTA

SPELLBOUND
from SPELLBOUND

Words by MACK DAVID
Music by MIKLOS ROZSA

With pedal

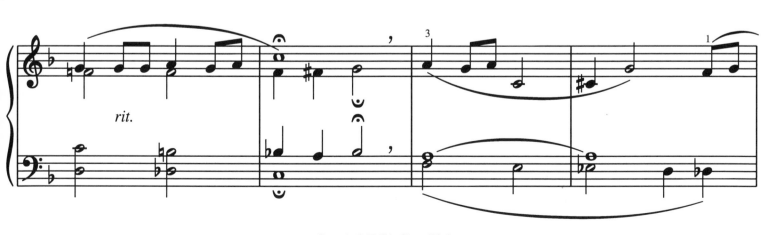

FORREST GUMP – MAIN TITLE

(Feather Theme)

from the Paramount Motion Picture FORREST GUMP

Music by ALAN SILVESTRI

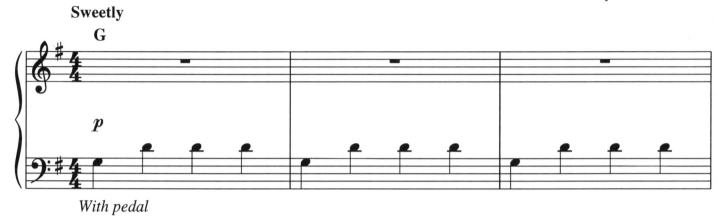

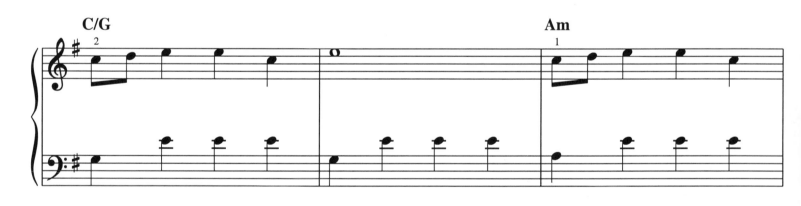

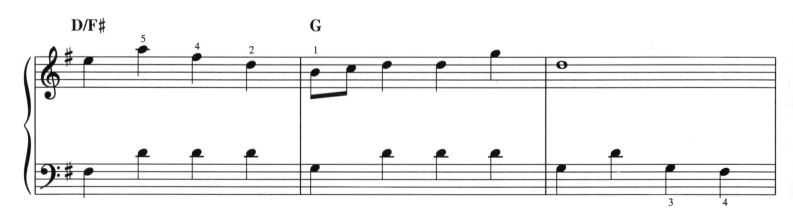

66

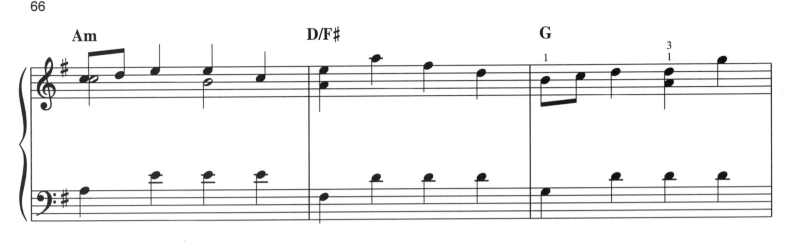

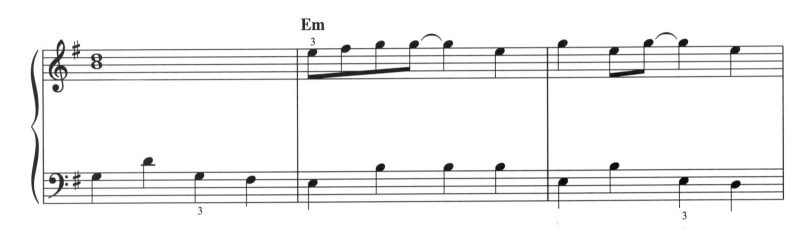

RAIDERS MARCH

from the Paramount Motion Picture RAIDERS OF THE LOST ARK

Music by JOHN WILLIAMS

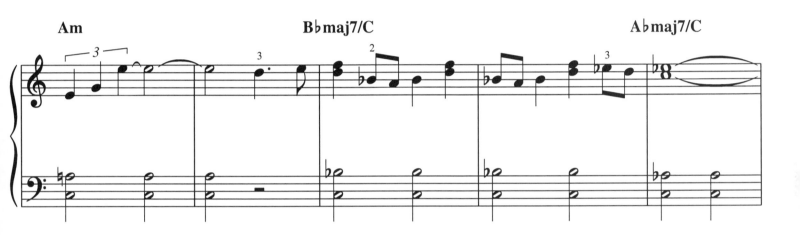

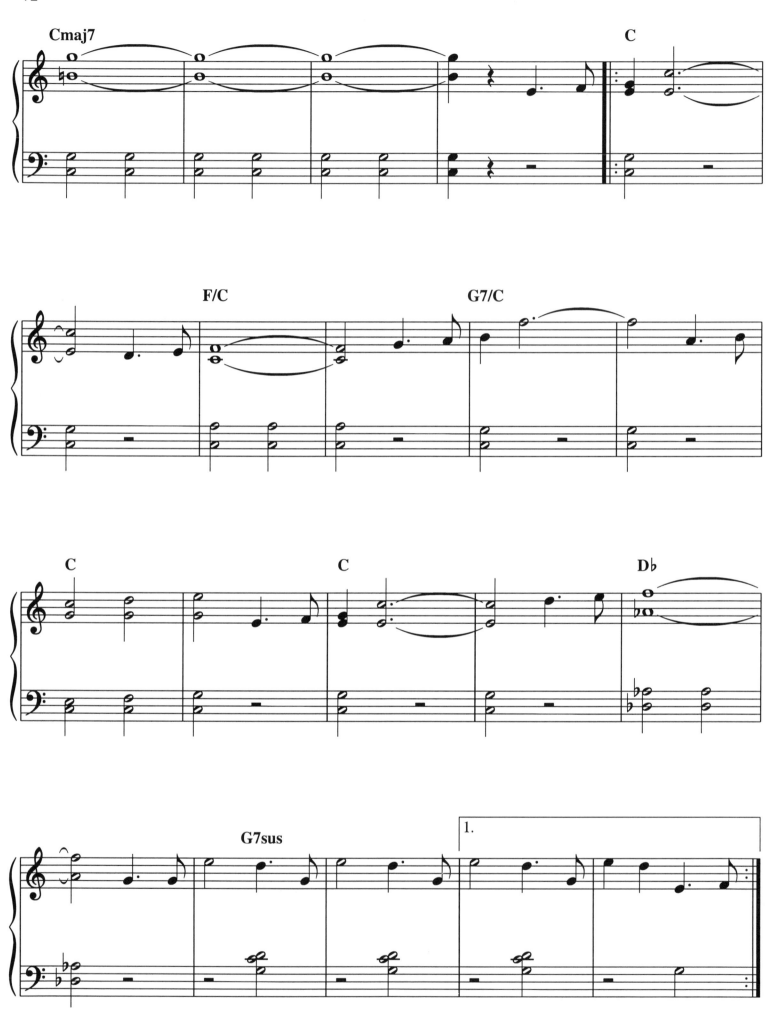

73

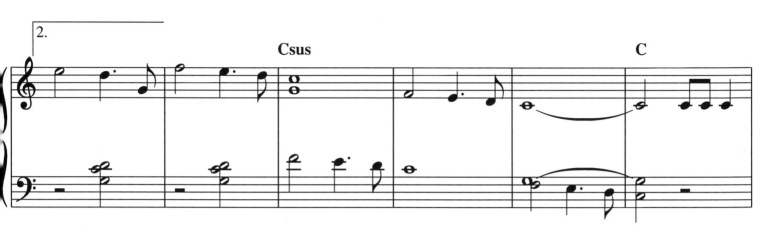

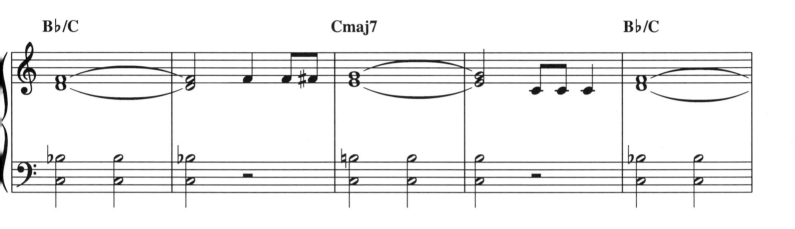

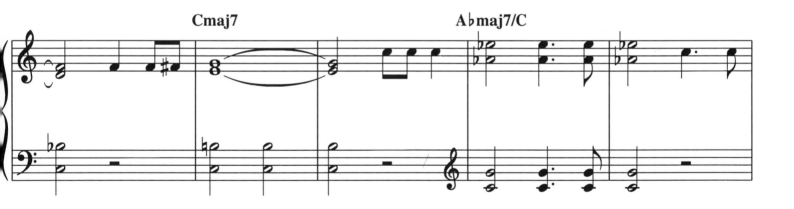

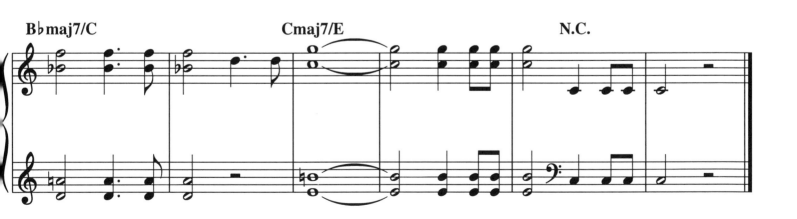

CHARIOTS OF FIRE

from CHARIOTS OF FIRE

Music by VANGELIS

THEME FROM ANGELA'S ASHES

Paramount Pictures and Universal Pictures International Present ANGELA'S ASHES

Music by JOHN WILLIAMS

Slow, gently flowing

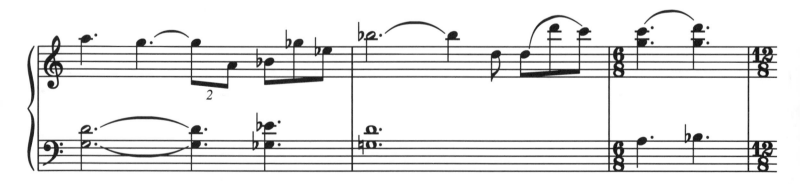

With motion

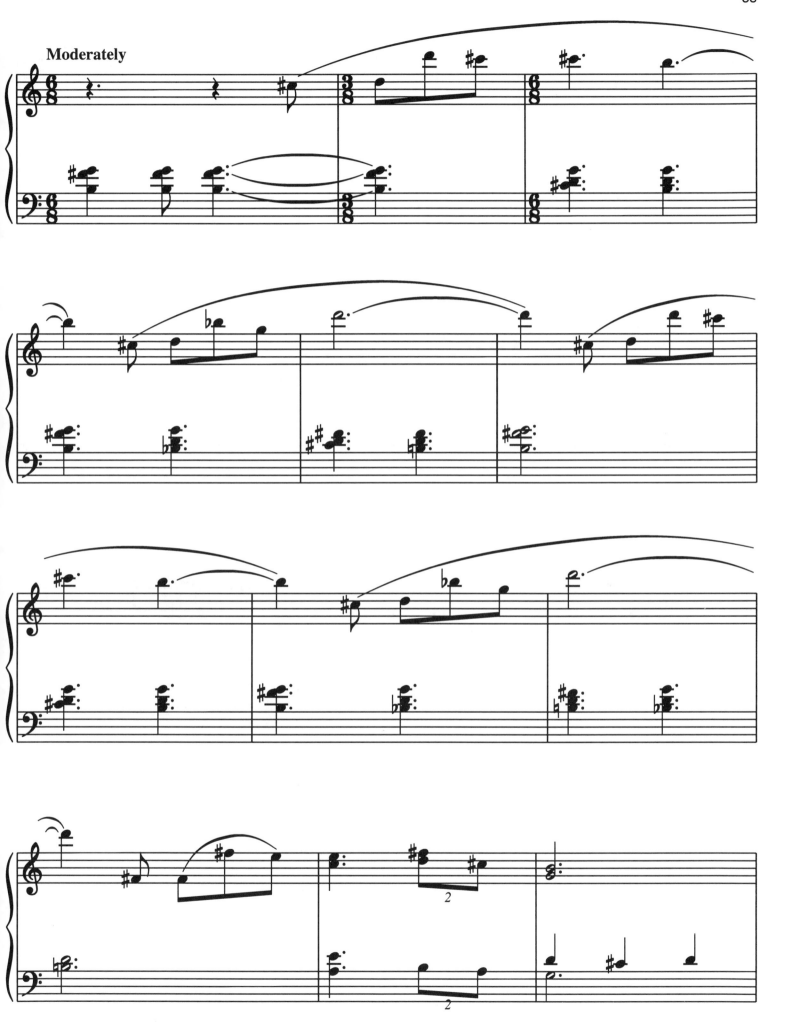

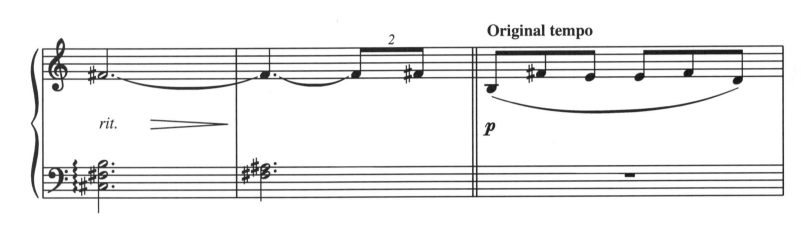

HYMN TO THE FALLEN
from the Paramount and DreamWorks Motion Picture SAVING PRIVATE RYAN

Music by JOHN WILLIAMS

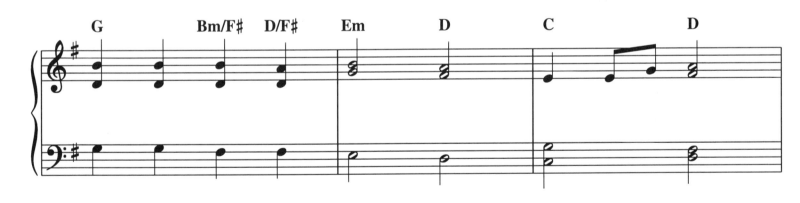

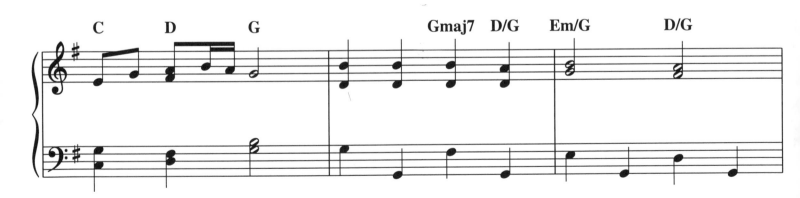

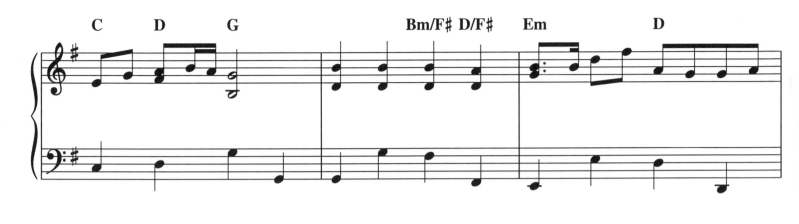

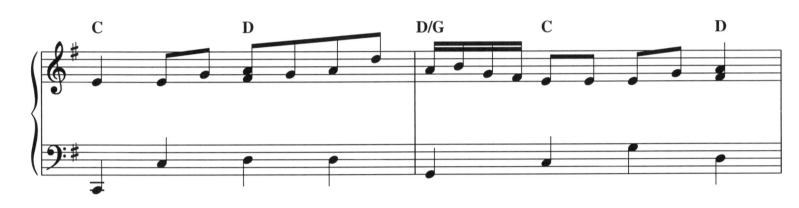

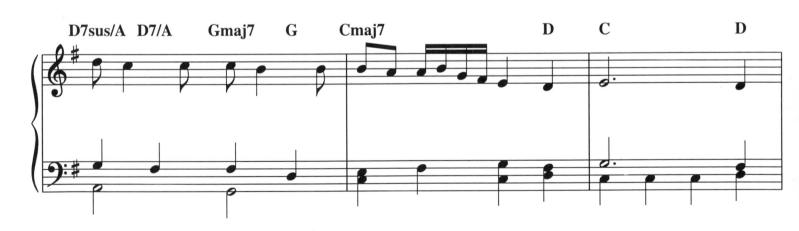

THE ENGLISH PATIENT
from THE ENGLISH PATIENT

Written by GABRIEL YARED

With expression and rhythmic freedom

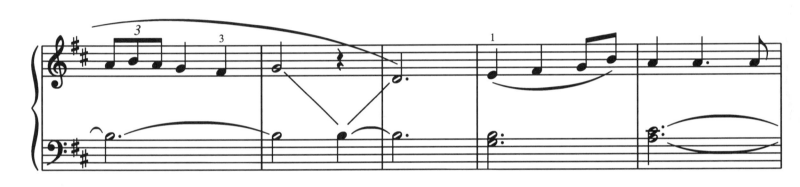